Math Around Us

D1224826

Playground Math

Dawn James

Cavendish Square

New York

Published in 2015 by Cavendish Square Publishing, LLC
243 5th Avenue, Suite 136, New York, NY 10016

First Edition

Website: cavendishsq.com

This publication represents the opinions and views of the author based on his or her personal experience, knowledge, and research. The information in this book serves as a general guide only. The author and publisher have used their best efforts in preparing this book and disclaim liability rising directly or indirectly from the use and application of this book.

CPSIA Compliance Information: Batch #WW15CSQ

All websites were available and accurate when this book was sent to press.

Library of Congress Cataloging-in-Publication Data

James, Dawn, author.
Playground math / Dawn James.
pages cm. — (Math around us)
Includes index.
ISBN 978-1-50260-152-0 (hardcover) ISBN 978-1-50260-150-6 (paperback) ISBN 978-1-50260-158-2 (ebook)
1. Counting—Juvenile literature. 2. Arithmetic—Juvenile literature. 3. Playgrounds—Juvenile literature. I. Title.

QA113.J372 2015
513.2—dc23

2014032627

Editor: Amy Hayes
Copy Editor: Cynthia Roby
Art Director: Jeffrey Talbot
Designer: Douglas Brooks
Senior Production Manager: Jennifer Ryder-Talbot
Production Editor: David McNamara
Photo Researcher: J8 Media

Printed in the United States of America

Contents

Going to the **playground** is lots of fun!

How many girls are on the swings?

2 girls are on the swings.

John swings across
3 monkey bars.

Then he swings across
2 monkey bars.

How many monkey bars has
John swung across?

He has swung across
5 monkey bars.

6

Shirley plays **hopscotch**.

She hops **5** squares, and then she hops **3** more.

What number will Shirley land on?

Shirley will land on the number **8**.

The **carousel** goes around and around.

How many kids are on this carousel?

5 kids are on the carousel.

4 kids are on a tire swing.

3 kids get off.

How many kids are still on the tire swing?

1 kid is on the tire swing.

Keisha loves to play with her **Hula-Hoop**.

She twirls it **4** times, and then **2** more times.

Keisha twirled her Hula-Hoop **6** times.

Steve and his mom play for **2** hours.

Then they play another hour.

How many hours have they played?

They have played for **3** hours.

The seesaw moves up and down.

How many kids are on the seesaw?

2 kids are on the seesaw.

How many kids are on
the slide?

5 kids are on the slide.

Learning at the playground
is fun.

New Words

carousel (KARE-o-sell) A circular platform that goes around in a circle.

hopscotch (HAWP-skawch) A game in which you hop on numbers drawn on the ground.

Hula-Hoop (HOO-la HOOP) A round, plastic toy that is twirled around the body.

monkey bars (MON-key BARS) Bars on which children swing.

playground (PLAY-grownd) An outdoor area where kids play.

Index

About the Author

Dawn James loves taking photographs and going to baseball games. She lives in Pittsburgh, Pennsylvania.

About BOOKWORMS

Bookworms help independent readers gain reading confidence through high-frequency words, simple sentences, and strong picture/text support. Each book explores a concept that helps children relate what they read to the world they live in.